70 Things
First-time Home Buyers
Need To Know

To the adventurous of us over fifty who undertake new careers, successful or not.

To the four sweet ladies in my new family, who put up with an old dog who resists learning new tricks.

70 Things
First-time Home Buyers
Need To Know

Jim Kimmons

TRADE PAPER
PRESS

Trade Paper Press
An imprint of Turner Publishing Company
Nashville, Tennessee
www.turnerpublishing.com

70 Things First-time Home Buyers Need To Know

Library of Congress Cataloging-in-Publication Data
ISBN 9781596526006 (paperback)

Printed in the United States of America

10 11 12 13 14 15 16 17—0 9 8 7 6 5 4 3 2

I want a house that has got over all its troubles; I don't want to spend the rest of my life bringing up a young and inexperienced house.

—Jerome K. Jerome, British author and humorist

Contents

Introduction

This is a book about decisions. You've made one by picking it up and checking out this introduction. You may have already made the decision to buy it. But the most important thing to me is for this book to remove as much as possible any chance of you making home-purchase decisions in a vacuum. Knowledge and information can fill that vacuum and empower you to make informed decisions.

I looked through several recent real estate purchase transactions in which I represented the buyers. In going through the pile of contracts, inspections, offers, counter offers, title insurance documents, and more, I found that I could easily count more than 100 decision points for my buyers in every one of them. That's a lot of decisions, especially if it's your first time to buy a home.

Whether you're a first-time home buyer or you've done it before but want to know more about the process, this is my opportunity to share my knowledge and experience as a realtor with you. And it's a thrilling opportunity for me on many levels.

The single most exciting thing for me is the chance to share information you may not get elsewhere but should know. I'm proud to be a real estate professional, and I'm lucky to be able to help people realize their dream of home ownership. The vast majority of real estate agents and mortgage professionals have the same attitude. But it's a business in which there are a lot of no-payday situations if the buyer doesn't make it through closing.

If you're given this book by a real estate or mortgage professional, it indicates that he or she isn't afraid to tell you what you need to know. It shows a true desire to empower you with knowledge to make great decisions, not have them made for you.

This book also gives you complete information that could allow you to take a path that may not be the easiest for the real estate agent. It may make his or her job harder. It could mean a deal falling through because you took a hard negotiation line. Or, because of something you learn here, you may decide to cease negotiations due to disclosures or issues you discover in documents.

If you bought the book, then you're to be congratulated for your planning and the thought you're putting into this most major of purchases in your life. I won't let you down. When you've read this book, you'll have a thorough knowledge of the process, from the home search through the closing and beyond.

The 70 Things

− 1 −
Should you buy or rent?

Since you're reading this book, your plan includes buying a home soon. But maybe you're second-guessing your decision, or reading in the media that it may be better now to rent than to buy.

The problem with articles about rent-versus-buy is that most of the discussion is about the "investment" in a home, and whether you'll experience appreciation or depreciation in value. And that's a valid concern. But we invest more than just money in our home. Where we live, how we live, and how much we enjoy our lives can be influenced greatly by our home environment. Are you unhappy with limitations on what you can do in a rental home? Would you love to paint one room orange but can't?

How about the proximity of noisy neighbors in an apartment or rental condo? If you don't have any private outdoor space, how important is that to you? Are you paying rent that could be a house note and settling for older appliances, nosy landlords, and the problems that accompany them? There are just too many lifestyle preferences that should enter into your decision to buy or to rent.

Even if you're not in an apartment but a single-family home, have you been forced to move because the owner decided to sell? It happened twice in a row to someone I know. He actually liked the homes he was renting and did not like moving around. The problem was that he'd just get settled in, even signing eighteen-month leases, only to have two homes in a row put on the market before the lease was up. He bought a home so he could be secure in his location. It's not all about just investment. In fact, read the next item to get a clear picture of your home's value as a place to enjoy life, and as an investment. It's still the American dream to own your own home.

— 2 —
Your home is not a
retirement investment

No matter how many advertisements you see on
TV or ads you read in newspapers or maga-
zines that tell you it is, your home should not be
counted on as a retirement investment. For every
homeowner who will tell you they increased their
net worth during the boom years of home price
increases, there are five more who ended up with a
home worth less than they paid for it, or even worse,
a foreclosure. A large number of those were purchased at the top of a frenzied market, not using the
tools and knowledge you'll get in this book.

Your home should be all about where and how
you live, enjoying life, and locating where you and
your family can enjoy the best and most economical
lifestyle. Then, take any excess money and invest it

in other ways to fund your retirement. One of those other investment choices could be real estate, but every property you buy for investment is selected based on very different considerations than your primary residence.

Your home should be selected based on your jobs, schools, and lifestyle choices for entertainment, outdoor activities, and cultural interests. In other words, choose a home based on enjoying your home and life. Don't buy at the top of your affordability scale simply because it's in a neighborhood you think will appreciate.

Homes can go up in value, and be happy if yours does. But they're not a liquid investment. You can't sell one like a share of stock with a phone call or the click of a mouse. It can take months, and the costs to sell are nothing like a stock transaction commission. It takes longer and costs a lot more, and you still have the risk that you won't come out with more than you put into the home. Just don't go into the purchase process treating it like an investment in future financial security. I've owned several homes, and it's what I want in my life. I hate renting and the restrictions it places on enjoying my home.

In January 2010, a *New York Times* article printed a graph with statistics showing that median home prices, adjusted for inflation, were the lowest since 1997. And there had not been a year when median home prices rose since 2005. Sure, a long period of rising prices preceded this five-year decline, but don't count on being able to buy at the bottom and sell higher. Over time, a home has been a pretty good investment, definitely better than throwing rent down a hole. Just see it as where you live, not a 401(k).

I wouldn't want to live any other way. Owning my home is a must. I just don't intend to count on it for a retirement income down the road.

– 3 –

Be selling when you're buying

Being aware that your home is where you live, and your retirement investments are somewhere else, is smart. I don't want to sound like I'm contradicting the "not-a-retirement-investment" advice, but the one forward-looking thing you must do when buying your first home is to think about selling it. Though you don't want to be lulled into believing your home will secure your retirement, you do want to buy with future resale in mind. It's just not common sense to ignore the potential for future appreciation, or the negative alternative.

The types of things you need to consider at buying time have to do with obvious area and market conditions, how an area is developing or deteriorating, and what has happened to home values in that neighborhood historically. Your real estate agent can be helpful here. One thing you want to watch out for are businesses closing nearby, which could indicate a neighborhood with job losses and a declining population. If there are two homes that are comparable in price and features you want and the locations are both acceptable, choosing the one in an area that's historically done well in value appreciation may be the way to go.

I am a working real estate broker in a mountain vacation home market, but the things to consider about area are much the same as in an urban subdivision. My clients expect me to help them with information about how an area has appreciated over time in relation to other areas. Even if the entire market has been down a bit, there are always some areas that aren't down as much, and some of those areas go up more in value in good times.

All other things being equal, think like you're selling when you're buying. How would other buyers, even those with different family and job characteristics, look at this home and neighbor-hood? It's not a retirement investment, but that doesn't mean you shouldn't consider it a major long-term investment in your lifestyle that you'd like to see worth more than you have in it when you sell.

— 4 —

Kitchens can be remodeled—
neighborhoods are harder

Many real estate agents much prefer selling homes to selling vacant land. Land requires the ability to help the buyers visualize what it could look like some day with their home on it. That's not nearly as easy as letting the couple into a home and having one of them fall in love with the gourmet kitchen. That agent can just stand there and soak in all the "Oh, it's wonderful!" statements, and all of the talk of the great parties they'll have once they're in the home.

Factoring something like this into your decision is okay, but the "falling-in-love" process should start from the exterior and move inward, not the other way around. Is the neighborhood a place you would be eager to come home to every day? Can you see yourself taking walks or enjoying other outdoor activities near home?

If your decision is more about distance to work and you aren't as concerned about neighborhood, you may be willing to trade off neighborhood for gas and time savings, going straight into your home every evening and not venturing out except by car.

The thing to remember is that kitchens can be remodeled with all of the latest "gotta-haves." Remodeling a neighborhood can take decades, and there are too many cooks in that kitchen. Look long and hard at the area, and be sure that you will enjoy living there for a number of years.

— 5 —
Condo or single-family home?

Should you buy a condominium instead of a detached single-family home? There are certainly some appealing features and benefits in owning a condo:

- No yard work or exterior maintenance, not a small thing in today's busy world.
- Lower cost of insurance: you insure the interior, and your condo fees cover exterior insurance.
- More savings come from trash, water, sewer, and possibly other services that are part of the homeowner fees and are discounted based on the number of units in one location. Condo associations can sometimes negotiate discounts from vendors for single-location volume accounts.
- They can be located in premium urban locations

that would require much higher home costs for houses with their own lots.

- Common-area amenities that can include a club-house, pool, exercise facility, and more.

Just be ready for some limitations of ownership with condominiums. The restrictions on what you can and cannot do can be annoying. Owners are almost always highly restricted in what they can do to change the exterior of their units. In many cases, those restrictions move into the interior as well. It's important to remember that you've bought into group ownership of sorts. You do own your unit, but you will be required to live within the rules the group has set up in order to maintain property values and a uniform look and feel for the project.

Your single vote in condo association meetings is important but will rarely tip the scales in a vote on something of great concern to you. Raising fees and special assessments to fix roofs or maintain exteriors and common areas will come about, even if you don't agree.

Failing to pay assessments or violations of rules and covenants can result in liens against your unit which, even if you avoid temporarily, will get paid in the sale of the unit in the future.

There are good reasons to choose condo living, but be careful to read all covenants, rules, and financial statements before ever considering an offer to buy. If the financial documents don't show a strong financial picture, think twice. Also, read documents carefully to catch planned future assessments that could amount to thousands of dollars. You don't want one of these to surprise you in your first couple of years of ownership.

Though detached single-family home values are influenced by neighborhood, you can make decisions about your home that can make it stand out from the others nearby. With a condominium, your ability to make changes is hampered, and you are very dependent on group decisions. If a poor economy, like the period from 2006 into 2010, causes depressed home prices, it will be much more difficult for you to help your situation if you're in a condo. Your fate is highly dependent on the group.

– 6 –

The cheapest home in the neighborhood could be the best one to buy

Here we're thinking again about selling while we're buying. There are always neighborhoods that seem to be just where everyone wants to live, for a number of reasons related to home styles, location, outdoor activities, or just the views. Regardless, they're the neighborhoods where people want to be.

If you have a desire to be there as well and can afford to be there without stressing your budget, you may want to think about buying the smallest home in the area, or the one that is "view challenged." It is usually the lowest-priced home in that area and will likely always be near that low-priced position even if all the homes appreciate in value, as it still has the characteristics that set it apart in the first place.

Experienced real estate agents and investors will tell you that there is always a group of buyers who desire to live in an area, but can't quite afford it. If they can locate a home in that neighborhood that's in the buyer's price range, whatever its size or challenges, it's usually an easy sale. They want to be there, and that's the only home they can afford. Keep this in mind, and be selling when you're buying.

– 7 –

Energy efficiency: ask for it

If you're looking at existing homes, you may end up purchasing the right home with the wrong appliances or heating and air-conditioning equipment. If you are aware of this and willing to upgrade for efficiency later, then no problem. But if you're not at least asking about energy efficiency, letting your agent and builders know that it's important to you, they'll keep showing you only what you do ask about.

If you keep talking about soaking tubs, skylights, granite counters, and things like that, then they will make those important in their selection of which homes to show you. But if you always mention high-efficiency appliances and comfort systems as just as important, you'll be looking at homes that will be more affordable for you down the road. There's also the good feeling you get from knowing that you've reduced your "carbon footprint," something good for the environment. But it's even better when it results in spending a lot less money every month to heat and cool the home and to heat water.

– 8 –

Before the search, get prequalified

You're getting excited and are probably all over the Internet looking at homes and searching neighborhoods. That's great, and I'll help you to find the most accurate, up-to-date, and complete listing information. But before any serious searching, you should visit one or more lenders or mortgage brokers and get prequalified for a mortgage.

This accomplishes a couple of very important things. First, you learn about mortgages, things like adjustable rates and fixed loans, and you learn which will best fit your financial situation and ability to make those payments. Second, you'll learn how much home you can buy. When the mortgage markets crashed in 2007 through 2009, loans became more difficult to get. Credit score requirements were raised, and down payments went up. Unlike the heady days that created the crash, nowadays lenders are quite careful to qualify you only for what you can afford.

So why would you want to be searching listings at prices far above what you can finance? It's a letdown to find out the homes you've been putting on your A-list are out of your reach. Go to several lenders, provide them with the income and financial information they need, and you'll find out the price range you need to be searching. You'll also need to get a preapproval letter that most real estate agents will advise you to have before submitting an offer. The seller in today's market is going to give more consideration to an offer that comes with a letter stating you can get the deal financed.

Very important: don't sign up for an online service that submits your information to a whole lot of lenders with a promise that they'll compete for your business. At least don't let them check your credit; a number of credit checks within a short period of time can have a negative impact on your score.

– 9 –

Mortgage basics

There's no need to study to become a mortgage broker to buy your first home. But it helps if you know a few things about mortgages before you go into a lender's office or visit a mortgage broker.

Fixed rate mortgages

These mortgages are set up with an interest rate that doesn't change during the life of the loan. Whether fifteen years, thirty years, or some other mortgage length, the interest rate will stay the same. This is the most popular mortgage type, as the borrower knows what his payments will be, and the principal and interest payment amount will not change.

Adjustable rate mortgages (ARMs)

In an ARM, the interest rate is adjusted over time. This was a very popular loan during the home price high-flying years up to 2006, mainly because it allowed some buyers to qualify for a larger home by reducing the interest rate and payment for the first one to five years, sometimes even ten years. An early rate is set up that's lower than a fixed rate because the lender knows they can raise the rate at some point if overall interest rates have gone up. It increases their return on the investment, as compared to a fixed loan that locks them in for the life of the loan. The problem comes when rates go up and the adjustment date rolls around, bringing a payment increase that's not in your budget.

If interest rates are at historic lows, adjustable rate mortgages can put the buyer at risk. If they go up, and the adjustment rolls around, the home-owner's payments will go up with the new higher interest rate. Some buyers are expecting a promotion on the job in a year or so, and see a chance to get a larger home with an ARM. That's okay if you're able to accept the consequences of that promotion not happening and your house payment going up as well.

Special payment plans to cut interest

Some buyers who can afford to take out a fifteen-year mortgage instead of a thirty-year loan will pay a higher monthly payment but will pay the home off in half the time and save a *huge* chunk of interest. But most first-time home buyers aren't too keen on this, nor can they afford the higher payment. There are other ways that can work for you, such as sending in extra principal payments now and then, or setting up to pay every two weeks. This biweekly payment option ends up with thirteen payments each year instead of twelve, which can pay the loan off as much as eight years sooner, saving a lot of interest as well.

MIP (mortgage insurance premium)

Whenever a buyer doesn't have at least a 20 percent down payment, there is a good chance that there will be an extra up-front or monthly addition (or both) to the payment for mortgage insurance. The lender has a higher amount loaned on the property and thus wants insurance to cover the mortgage if you default. Generally, you'll get to kill the additional payment premium when your equity hits 20 percent. These fees come and go and change, so ask your lender or mortgage broker about your exposure and costs.

— 10 —
Selecting a mortgage broker or lender

The aftermath of the home price and mortgage market near-collapse has encouraged some mega-banks, like Bank of America and Wells Fargo, to try to work more directly with borrowers via their branches and Web sites. This direct approach can save the borrower money at closing, as there isn't a mortgage broker between you and the lender.

The drawback of the direct approach is that you'll be dealing with a lender with certain loan products and rates, and they'll not be very flexible in these offerings. A mortgage broker, at least a good one, will be working with some of these same lenders, but also others, to locate the best loan and terms for your situation. This is particularly true if you have credit problems that may need to be corrected or worked around.

Also, you'll probably have to be even more selective among mortgage brokers if you want to take advantage of Homepath, USDA, or other creative mortgages because some brokers will simply have no experience with them and may not want that type of business.

~ 11 ~
Mortgage fees are negotiable

This isn't a blanket statement, but most of the time you can negotiate with mortgage brokers on the up-front fees they control. Points for loan origination and other fees can add thousands of dollars to your up-front costs. You're bringing business to the mortgage broker, so don't feel in the least fearful about asking for lower fees.

The lender will give you a "good faith estimate" and "truth in lending disclosure" that outlines the expected fees and your costs in getting the home closed. One of the items that confuses buyers is the APR, or annual percentage rate. You are told that you'll be getting a loan at an interest rate of 6.5 percent, but you see 6.875 percent in the APR box.

That's because the lender must factor in fees to give you a better way to compare loans.

You can get three lenders quoting the same 6.5 percent mortgage rate, but three different APRs. This tells you something about the fees being added into the closing, and makes comparisons easier. Your long-term mortgage rate is still the 6.5 percent, but the APR just factors in up-front fees. These fees include all kinds of title fees, some closing costs, and any up-front mortgage insurance premiums paid at closing.

— 12 —

Escrow and how it works

Unless you're paying cash for a property, it's likely that the lender will want to escrow money for the payment of property taxes and insurance. They get a certain amount up front at closing to cover the first six months or year of insurance premiums and expected taxes. Then an amount is added to each payment to build up the escrow over time, as these premiums and taxes are being paid for you out of this escrow fund. This protects the lender from losing the property if an owner doesn't pay these important items on time.

Because an estimate of the escrow is one of your up-front lending items and part of your monthly payment, you'll want a firm handle on what that will be. As insurance and taxes change, so might the amount added to your payment for escrow. There are laws limiting how much escrow a lender can hold back, so they may even end up giving you a downward adjustment if payouts are less than anticipated. You should get annual statements of the amount you have in escrow, letting you know whether more or less needs to be collected in your payments.

– 13 –

Know what's going to happen with real estate taxes

Though there will be money placed in an escrow account to pay future real estate taxes, you want to be sure you have a reasonable expectation of what those taxes will be. In most urban areas it's probable that assessments of homes are reasonably up-to-date. Thus, the buyer can expect that the taxes, at least for the first year of ownership, will be approximately what's being placed in escrow.

But be aware if the assessments aren't up-to-date. Rural and smaller counties can be years behind in assessing home values. So after closing, the price is reported to the county, and that may become the tax value. If the escrow is for last year's tax amount charged to the previous owner, you could end up without enough in escrow to pay the new taxes, resulting in a bill sent to you to add money to escrow and an increase in monthly payments to keep escrow properly funded.

Every state, and sometimes even different counties, can vary with their assessments and taxes, so just be sure to know what to expect, especially if a valuation increase is coming right away.

The best available mortgage
for most of us

The FHA (Federal Housing Administration), even after the mortgage problems beginning in 2007, was tasked by the government to keep housing affordable and to help spur home sales by keeping mortgage money available to those without 20 percent down payments.

Policies and requirements change with the wind, so check with your lender for current FHA loan guarantee requirements. At the time of this writing, 3.5 percent down payments were still available, though the bottom credit score was raised, and mortgage insurance premiums were going up as well. The mortgage failures beginning in 2007 created a financial crisis for the FHA, and credit requirements were raised to lower risk. However, it's still the most likely mortgage option for the down-payment challenged to take advantage of.

— 15 —
If you're rural, the USDA could be your best friend

A gain, things change, but there's been a loan program around for a good while that provides guaranteed loans for home buyers from an unexpected source: the U.S. Department of Agriculture. It is a program designed to help buyers in rural areas who may not have the mortgage sources available in larger cities.

It gets even better. This program will back a loan of up to 103 percent of the appraised value of the home! As closing costs are usually more in the neighborhood of 5 percent to 6 percent, there's still cash out of pocket required to close the deal. That's unless you get yourself preapproved for this loan and make an offer requiring the seller to pay up to 3 percent of closing costs.

This isn't a pie-in-the-sky deal, as I just helped a single mother of three to buy her home through this offer without any down payment. She even got her $500 earnest money deposit back at closing, and all inspection and appraisal fees paid for her as well. The seller paid half the closing costs, and the loan took care of the rest. Check it out at USDA.gov.

16

Homepath—your path to a foreclosure home purchase

One of the greatest hurdles to home buyers in taking advantage of foreclosure bargains has been the condition of the home and the repairs necessary to get it into the livable condition required by lenders. Many foreclosure homes have been stripped of cabinets, doors, appliances, and even toilets. At one point, the average buyer had no way to get a mortgage, as they couldn't put their money into rehabbing the home before they even owned it. Many times investors have purchased them, doing the work and marking up the price for a nice profit.

There is now a way for the average buyer, even the first-time home buyer, to purchase a foreclosure, have all repairs made before closing, and have those repair costs financed into the mortgage. It's the

Homepath program from Fannie Mae. The program makes available specific foreclosure homes held and preapproved by Fannie Mae. Go to the site at www.HomePath.com for a national map, and search by state to find qualifying homes in your area.

17

The truth about short sales

The mortgage meltdown beginning in 2007 made the term "short sale" very popular in Google searches. Whether it involved a homeowner looking for a way to avoid foreclosure, or an investor wanting to buy below market value and mortgage balance, short sales were big news.

Simply put, a short sale happens when a lender accepts a purchase price on a home that's less than the amount the homeowner owes on the mortgage. They're accepting a "short" payoff. Though it will still damage a homeowner's credit, it's generally thought to be better than going into foreclosure.

One would think that if the purchase price wasn't so far below the mortgage balance to be ridiculous, that the bank would accept it to avoid the legal hassle and costs of foreclosure. The hard fact is that according to one report, in the heyday of short sale offers, only about 20 percent of those offers made it to closing. Reasons given in the report for the low percentage included:

- Banks weren't ready or staffed for the volume of those making the offers.
- Some lenders actually preferred the control of a foreclosure.
- Borrowers and their buyers didn't do a good job with paperwork and convincing the lender that the short sale was their best option.

It's all guesswork, and all of these reasons have merit. But the important thing to know as a buyer is that it's really a tough road to get from a short sale offer to a closing. And you're in a time crunch, as the process is moving steadily toward bankruptcy or foreclosure.

A large percentage of deals never closed simply because the buyers gave up. After months of wrangling with the lender, they still couldn't get a deal sealed. Not wanting to pass up a good buying market, they simply withdrew their offers and walked away. If you still want to try to buy a home from a homeowner in mortgage trouble through a short sale, at least you're aware of the issues. For that 20 percent who are successful, it's still a long haul to a short sale.

– 18 –
Getting home-listing information on the Web

O kay, you've learned the mortgage ropes, know what you can afford, and are ready to do some serious online research. It's definitely the way to go, and just about everything you want to know is on the Web . . . just about. Let's talk about some well-known Web sites and how they work.

Realtor.com

This is the big daddy of real estate listing Web sites, stating that it has all of the member realtor listings for the entire country. The listings are automatically fed to Realtor.com from local member Multiple Listing Services, so they are very up-to-date. But Realtor.com then takes the information from the MLS and modifies it to fit their format, sometimes eliminating or rewording information fields. There's also favoritism in the order they're displayed based on several factors that may not result in the best homes for you appearing at the top of the list. Regardless, it's the single Web site with the most listings out there.

Zillow, Trulia, and others

Even Google is getting into the listing business on the Web, so there are a great many sites to look at homes for sale. Although Realtor.com is usually the most up-to-date, as listings are automatically added and removed with feeds from local Multiple Listing Services, there's some good information to be gleaned from comparing the same home listing among Realtor.com, Zillow.com, and Trulia.com. There may be some fields of information on one that aren't available on another.

IDX: the best local resource

All of those megasites boast a million or more listings all around the country. That's great if you're about to buy a home in every state, but you're just buying one, and in one location. So if you can find a local real estate site that has all of the local listings in the Multiple Listing Service, that would be a good resource.

Real estate brokers are members of local Multiple Listing Services, and they have various agreements and rules in place in order to share their home listing information online, as well as how they'll split commissions when other members bring a buyer.

IDX, or Internet Data Exchange, is an agreement among broker members of an MLS to share their listings, with every broker's listings available in a search on any of their Web sites. This gives you the most complete and up-to-date listing resource for most areas. But you will only see the information fields that the brokers have agreed upon, and it'll be the same on every site. For example, my MLS doesn't put the acreage with a home in the IDX search. In fact, there are many fields of detail that aren't available in the IDX search display, but getting to a local broker's site that has IDX is still the best local-listing search approach. Now take a look at the next item in this book for what you need to know to get those missing information fields.

– 19 –

Getting full home information delivered as it happens

Most of the MLS software systems today allow an agent to set a buyer up with a custom search. Your desired home characteristics are entered in the system, which will deliver you an e-mail when any broker in that MLS enters a new listing matching your needs. You'll also get price change notifications, so you can keep an eye on homes you like that need to come down in price before they hit your target. And they can send you more detailed listing displays, usually with more fields of information on each listing.

Some agent sites will actually let you build your own custom search, but many will just offer you a form to enter your home requirements in order for the agent to build your search. If you don't see either option, send an e-mail to ask the agent if they can do this for you. They should be able to.

Agents have what many call a "hot sheet" report that they are supposed to look at daily to catch new listings, expiring listings, and price changes. No matter how diligent an agent is in checking their hot sheets, they can't catch every listing suitable for every prospect, or changes made daily by all brokers in the MLS. Getting the system to deliver them to you automatically will actually get you "in the know" before most of the agents in town.

The value of this setup is best illustrated by a real-life example. I work in a resort and vacation home market, where local tourism employees have a really tough time finding affordable housing. One of my artist clients set up my automated alerts to keep an eye out for homes in her price range. She began to follow price changes on a few homes that were still out of her reach, but getting closer.

One of the homes she was watching, a foreclosure, sold for well over $200,000 in better economic times. It foreclosed and was listed at just over $200k. She just waited and watched the alerts for several months. The price dropped four times and finally reached her range. She acted the same day, which was a smart move. We submitted a contract and negotiated a deal just before several backup offers came in when other agents caught the price drop in their hot sheets. By the way, the price was *well* below that original $200k list price.

– 20 –
How Web listings can be incorrect—or not for sale at all

A major reason I suggest that the majority of your Web home searches be done on MLS IDX sites of local real estate brokers is because of accuracy and timeliness of the information. Realtor.com gets its feeds directly from the MLS's, and is generally pretty accurate, though it can be a day or two behind.

Other sites get their listings in a number of ways, including direct input by real estate agents, from tax records or other county deed records, or even homeowners entering their own listings. They can also be getting their listings from "syndication" of data entered on another site. The syndication site takes one entry from a real estate agent and sends it to the other sites.

The only problem here is that sometimes listings sell, but the agent forgets to remove them from one or more of the many sites where they're displayed. This results in listings of properties that aren't for sale, and upset new home owners who don't like the idea of their just-purchased home still being listed as for sale on Web sites.

Why would a MLS IDX site be different? All Multiple Listing Services hold their members to certain standards and rules. If I don't take a listing off the MLS within forty-eight hours of it going under contract, I'm subject to disciplinary action and a fine. The same applies going the other direction. If I get a new listing, I must get it onto the MLS within a tight deadline period or be fined.

Human nature is to make mistakes, so even MLS IDX search sites aren't perfect. One notable situation I see all of the time is listing agents who forget to contact their sellers and renew a listing before the expiration date. The system automatically "expires" and removes it on that date, so the agent receives a notice and contacts the seller. It can take a few days or more to get it back onto the MLS, and a day or so more before it hits Realtor.com.

So feel free to use multiple sites of all types to search for homes and information about markets. But remember that there may be listings that no longer exist, and there may be listings not there that will reappear in a few days. If one goes away to ex-piration, wait to see if it comes back.

– 21 –
Avoiding being referred until you're ready

One thing you can count on is that the money involved in real estate will draw huge numbers of "middle people" who want a share. And many of them want a significant share without providing value for it. Be careful of Web sites that want your information in exchange for services you're not yet ready for. Here's how these referral sites work:

- They offer information or services at no cost to you if you'll "register" and give your contact information.
- Many will ask for the specifics of your property needs, wanting to get as much detail as possible in exchange for a list of available homes.

- They will then "refer" you to real estate agents who have signed up and paid to get your information.

One problem for you is that you may end up with your information given to multiple agents. Then you're faced with mass e-mails and phone calls you don't want. Even if they give exclusive access to your information to only one of their agent subscribers, the agent paid for this "lead" and will want to get her money's worth. Now you're having to deal with an agent before you're ready, and not one you've had a chance to investigate before building a relationship. Another hard fact is that the more experienced and established agents usually will never pay for leads. They have their own systems in place, whether Web sites or networking, to get leads. So you may be getting the least experienced person, who must pay for leads to get customers until they're established.

Some very large, popular national Web sites of lenders and home listings sell your information to agents, and others take a portion of the agent's commission if you end up closing on a home from their lead. It's possible that you'll end up having a great experience if you work with an agent who got your information this way. Still, these kind of referrals are usually too early in the process, resulting in pressures and sales approaches long before you're ready.

– 22 –
Search a little higher asking price—you will be offering less

Many people believe that the days of fast home price appreciation will never come again. Whether or not they're right, people always believe their home is worth more than a stagnant or falling market will support. If they're adamant about a price, they can usually find a real estate agent to list it, even if it is overpriced for the current market.

There's also no way to know a seller's motivations and when they may change or become a little more desperate to sell. So when you set up your Internet searches, don't hesitate to use a price a little above what you think you can afford. You're not looking to buy those homes at their list prices. You're watching for price reductions and an opportunity to make a lower offer they may be willing to take.

– 23 –
Agents, brokers, associate and managing brokers?

Just knowing who you're working with and their position in the real estate "pecking order" can help you better understand how decisions are made and who may need to get clearance from others before they can promise something.

The term "real estate agent" is used to describe just about every real estate professional. But in most states, there is a hierarchy of experience or licensing. The law in many states is set up such that the agents are licensed under the supervision of a broker. The broker in these cases is responsible for the actions of their agents, and should have trained them before putting them on your deal.

Usually the agent is required to complete a certain amount of time in her profession, as well as satisfy education requirements, before she can test and license as a broker. Just because someone has many years in the business but is still an agent doesn't mean she isn't knowledgeable enough to be a broker. Many choose to stay agents because they don't want higher licensing fees, others working under them, or the responsibility for managing a brokerage office, and the extra paperwork that goes with it. They may also enjoy free marketing done by their broker, and negotiate better commission splits with them (see the next item).

In some states, everyone is a broker. This is relatively new, but it means that there are no "agents," with all of the licensees being "brokers." It relieves some of the liability from the broker running the office, but there are still usually time requirements for experience before those junior brokers can become full, managing, or sponsoring brokers in charge of others. Sometimes they have "Associate Broker" on their card.

Is a large office with lots of brokers or agents better for a buyer? Not really, as almost all real estate professionals are "independent contractors." This means they're all running their own mini-business inside of the brokerage, and competition is strong. Don't discriminate against a small brokerage or even a single-person office, as you're just as likely to get a great real estate professional there as you are in a big office.

- 24 -
How real estate agents get paid

There are new compensation arrangements cropping up all of the time in real estate, so those following in this section are just generalities. And since most of them originate from money paid by the seller that's split between the listing broker and the one working with you, it's all about the "splits." If an agent tells you that her services are free to you as a buyer, it's both a correct and an incorrect statement.

The seller is agreeing to a commission to be paid to her listing broker. It will be split at some percentage, usually down the middle, with the broker bringing you as a buyer. You aren't paying any money at closing labeled as a commission. But logically, if half of the commission the seller agreed to pay is for your agent, then the seller has factored this into their price. Essentially, you're paying for the service as part of the price of the home, so don't believe that you aren't a paying customer; you should be treated as one.

Here's how a $10,000 commission paid by a seller can be cut up before everybody gets a check.

- The listing broker offers a split to your agent's broker, usually 50 percent, so each broker is getting $5,000. Most state laws require that the broker get all money and distribute it to agents.
- The listing broker may even have a franchise fee coming off the top of their half.
- Then there is an agreement between the managing broker and their agents or associate brokers, on both buyer and seller sides, that specifies how they'll split the commission. It can be anything, but let's use a common 50 percent split here. So your agent is getting half of what their broker gets, or $2,500.

These percentages vary, with some major franchises dividing the cost differently, but you can see that your agent is at the end of a series of commission splits.

The seller is probably not thrilled to be paying $10,000 to get the home sold, but it's being split up among several companies and professionals to connect you with the seller's property and get the deal closed.

− 25 −
Who's your perfect real estate professional?

Every year, the National Association of Realtors surveys people who purchased homes the previous year. They ask a lot of questions about how they made decisions, how they found their realtor, and what they liked and didn't like about the process. One category in a recent survey asked first-time home buyers which benefits provided by the agent were the most valued. Here are the top three:

- Helped buyer understand the process
- Pointed out unnoticed features and faults with property
- Negotiated better sales contract terms

So it seems a safe conclusion to assume that these are things you want from a real estate professional as well. In my experience with buyers, and remembering their complaints to me about agents or their statements as to why I got the business, I would also offer the following tips and advice.

- When you e-mail an agent, you should get an answer within twenty-four hours, but it really should come in just a few hours.
- That answer shouldn't be a form e-mail about how "important your business is to them." It should be a real e-mail with an answer to your question.
- Serious professionals don't tell you they only work Monday through Friday . . . unless they have so much business they don't have time for you anyway.
- Information and answers to questions should be freely and quickly offered without a requirement to sign anything. At some point, you may sign an agreement, but you shouldn't have to do it early just to find out how the subdivision rules apply to the home you're interested in.

- Phone calls, e-mails, and text messages should be returned promptly, which shows they really do "value your business."
- They should know their market backward and forward, with statistics and information that is useful and can keep you out of trouble.
- They should be offering information about homes you view that helps you spot flaws and problems, not just the great features.

Don't make the easier information mistake!

I've had experienced buyers tell me that they prefer to deal directly with the listing agents, as they have all of the information about the home because they listed it. The buyer assumes that they'll get their questions answered faster and have a better flow in the transaction if they deal just through the listing agent.

The listing agent will be thrilled, as he'll be doubling his money, getting both the listing and the buying side of the commission. But getting rid of the small time lag in getting information directly, without a buyer agent on your side, may cost you a *lot* of money. If the listing agent is a true "agent" of the seller, he's signed a contract that pledges his full efforts to do his best for the seller, getting them the highest price possible for the property. Where do you stand in this arrangement? In a position to be paying more for the home than you should is where.

Even if the listing agent isn't a true "agent" of the seller, he has signed a contract with them to help them sell their home. Now you come along, and hand him the other side of the commission because you're dealing direct. The problems with human nature enter the picture, as there's now double the money involved, so how aggressive do you think your agent will be in helping you to discover any negative details in the house that could be used in an aggressive negotiation strategy? The more aggressive they are on your behalf, the greater the chance that the deal will blow up, and all of that double commission money will be gone.

To be fair, I and the majority of real estate professionals have handled both sides of many transactions. And I've always believed that I've given my best to both sides. But going into court with the same lawyer as the person you're suing isn't what you'd do, so think about that analogy when you're calling to get information on homes.

The very best of situations for you is to have your own buyer agent, not a member of the brokerage that has the listing, working aggressively to help you in getting every bit of information you can and negotiating the lowest price and best terms for your home purchase. Considering this chapter's advice, if a real estate agent gives you this book, he wants you to have this type of information, and that should give him a boost in your ethics selection category.

– 26 –
Agent referrals from friends or relatives

A t your first mention of your search for a home, especially when they know it's your first home purchase, your friends and family will be full of advice. They'll offer all sorts of suggestions as to the type of home you should buy, the location, and real estate professionals they've used in the past.

Their intentions are good, and your friends and relatives want you to be happy and make a successful first home purchase. Many times they're also responding to the popular practice of "working your past customers for referrals" used by most real estate agents. Postcards and other marketing materials always ask the client to make referrals. There's nothing wrong with the practice, and nothing wrong with using an agent referred by a friend or relative.

The National Association of Realtors' annual survey of home buyers and sellers always shows that a great many people, including first-time home buyers, used an agent referred to them by a friend, neighbor, or relative. But before you place your trust and information needs in the hands of a real estate professional, be sure to ask yourself some questions:

- If you're getting multiple referrals, and it's likely that you will, what criteria will you use if you want to work with one of the referred agents?
- Though well-meaning, did your friends and relatives have the same information needs as yours, or will you be buying in a different area, and a different type of home?
- Have there been changes in the lives or businesses of the agents being referred that could make them a less-than-optimal choice for your needs?
- Will you feel pressure not to hurt the feelings of a particular friend or family member by not taking her suggestion?

I'm not saying that a satisfied real estate client isn't a great source for a referral. But every customer is different with different needs, and home buying situations can vary in complexity or in problems with the transactions. This is probably going to be the single largest expenditure in your life thus far, so it's important for you to be the final decision-maker.

Your real estate agent can be the single most important service provider in the process. Their experience in the location and knowledge of problems homeowners have had there, as well as experience that helps them to notice and point out property problems, makes them a valuable resource.

Whether you work with a friend or family member's referred real estate professional, or you go out and do the research and find your own, it is most important that you really do the research. Choose based on reputation, and those referrals could be a part of that reputation piece. But a major part of your decision should be based on the real estate professional's knowledge and experience.

How free is an agent or broker with information, and how much do they share on their Web site or blog about the area and real estate? Can they give you statistics and help interpret them? Buying your first home is not an activity that should occur in a vacuum of local market information. The more numbers you analyze, and the more information you get, the more likely you'll be to make a decision that you'll be extremely happy with later.

- 27 -
Why you usually don't want to be referred agent-to-agent

A practice that's extremely popular in the real estate business is the referral of a client to another agent or brokerage in exchange for a percentage of the commission paid at closing. This referral fee percentage generally varies between 20 and 35 percent, depending on the agents and negotiation agreement.

Example: You happen to know an agent who doesn't work the area where you want to buy, but they ask if they can refer you to another agent in that area. In many states, there is no requirement that referral fees or their amount be disclosed to you. Either way, the agent who sends an e-mail with your contact information, about a ten-minute task, could get as much as a third of the commission of the agent who's about to do all of the real work, maybe for months.

Hot debates come about among real estate professionals as to whether referrals for money are ethical. But even dropping the ethical argument, let's look at human nature and the value added or not added in a referral situation. Even if you don't care whether the referring agent gets perhaps a couple thousand dollars for that e-mail, remember that this is money the agent on the other end, the one that's working with you, is giving up out of her commission.

If the referral goes to the brokerage, and they get to choose an agent to work with you, they may choose the newest person in the office with the least experience. This can happen for a lot of reasons, not the least of which is that the experienced and successful agents don't want to give up that percentage simply to get your business. They still do all of the work showing, negotiating, and taking you through to closing.

But even if you get a great agent, and even if they really care, can you count on getting your calls and e-mails answered as quickly as their full-commission clients? I have taken referrals of buyers and tried my very best to never put them lower on my priority list than a full-commission client. But that's the key: I had to really make it a priority, as human nature is to respond to the most "valuable" client first and fastest.

In general, unless you have a relative you would like to be highly compensated for adding little or no value to your deal, don't be "referred" for a fee.

– 28 –
Understanding agency and representation

Before you talk to any real estate agents or brokers, you should have a basic knowledge of the representation of buyers and sellers, as well as the duties of the agents. Because these are state laws in many cases, you'll need to check specifics in your state, but there are certain practices and representation types that are prevalent in many states.

There is still old consumer advice out there in the media that scares buyers by telling them that real estate agents working with a buyer work for the seller, and you shouldn't tell them anything you don't want the seller to know. The seller may be paying the commissions for both the listing and your buyer agent, but that doesn't mean that your agent is working for the seller. You would be hard-pressed to find many places in the country where this practice, called sub-agency, is still common. In sub-agency, the buyer's agent is working for the seller, so the agent can't do or say anything to hurt the seller's position . . . not a great situation for the buyer.

The new ways in which a buyer is represented usually allows his agent to aggressively represent his interests. Yes, the seller is offering a commission that is split between the broker listing the property for sale and the buyer agent who brings the buyer, but there is no requirement of any duties to the seller from the buyer agent except fairness, which is required of all parties.

I work only with buyers as a buyer broker, and I help them to negotiate hard, dig up all of the facts and property information—good or bad—and get the best deal they can. I never speak to or meet the seller and owe them nothing, even though I end up being paid out of the commission the seller agreed to with their listing broker.

Do you want an agent?

Though they're referred to as real estate agents by most people, there are not that many transactions in most states where the real estate professional is actually an "agent" of the buyer. The difference is legal, and mostly involves extra "fiduciary" duties to the client, including confidentiality and obeying their client's instructions.

Without getting into a lot of legalese, most states have a required disclosure form that your real estate professional must share with you before you become a client. It will explain their duties and may give you a choice as to whether you want them to be your "agent" or just a "buyer representative," broker, or "transaction facilitator." Any of the choices could be right for you. Most transactions done today are through "facilitator" or "brokerage" relationships without specified and contractual agency agreements. This is usually just fine for your needs as a buyer, but at the onset of the process, get an explanation from your agent and read disclosures carefully.

If a listing broker is a true "agent," with the fiduciary responsibilities to the seller that go along with it, then working with the buyer as well can present other issues. If you decide to work through the listing brokerage for your purchase, and they are an "agent" of the seller, then it must be asked if they're your "agent" as well.

How would this happen if you didn't set out wanting it? You found a great agent, and they've been wonderful in helping you to understand the market, showing you homes, and giving you information. Finally, you find the home of your dreams, and it's listed by your agent's brokerage. Now you're in a situation you didn't anticipate at the beginning of your search.

If they had you sign an agency agreement, and they're a true "agent" of the seller as well, then you'll end up in one of two situations, "dual" or "designated" agency. Dual agency means that your agent and his brokerage must now disclose their agency status with both you and the seller, and their role is to become no longer an agent for either. It's impossible to represent the best interests of both parties at the same time.

If dual agency exists, your agent and the listing agent will become "facilitators," moving paperwork and taking care of tasks related to getting the deal closed. But neither can be an agent anymore, so both clients get reduced services and representation from those promised in their agency agreements.

If "designated" agency is practiced by the brokerage, then one agent is assigned as your "agent." The other is assigned as the true "agent" of the seller. They each take on the duties of an agent for their clients, and they don't share information in any way. Each does their best for their client, solely representing their client's interests.

It's not the end of the world if you end up wanting to buy one of your agent's brokerage listings. Just understand the duties of everybody concerned in order to know what to expect in the way of services and loyalties.

— 29 —

"Buyers are liars," but it's changing

An old saying in the real estate industry is that "buyers are liars." This is partially a throwback to the days when buyer agents did work as sub-agents of the seller, and the buyer never wanted to tell the truth for fear it would be used against them in the negotiation. Then there's also the belief held by many that they will get "SOLD" something if they tell their agent the truth about what they can afford.

Using what you learn in this book, I believe that you'll choose a real estate professional who you can trust to work in your best interests to help you make a really great buy on your first home, and they'll need your help to do that. You can tell them what you're willing to pay or can afford. You shouldn't be concerned about being hustled or "sold up." Take charge—you're the customer and the boss, and your real estate professional is your service provider. Ask for their offer price advice, and balance it with market statistics they should be providing. But when it comes down to it, if they say you're making too low an offer, it's your call. If you're prepared to walk away without the home, then be as tough as you want in the negotiation.

It all comes down to selecting a real estate professional you can relate to and get along with, and one who will treat you as a valued customer who can make intelligent decisions if you're given all of the information you need. I can't tell you how many times I've said to a client: "Those are the comparable properties sold recently, and based on these numbers, I think this home is overpriced. But I'll make any offer you want me to." I usually say this to a client who has fallen in love with the home to the point of losing their objectivity. My job is to give them all of the information they need, then to do what they say.

It works the other way as well. When a client wants to "low-ball" an offer on a home, I can only give them my opinion backed up by recently sold home prices and current market conditions. If they say to low-ball it anyway, that's what we do. You want an agent who's not afraid to tell you the truth as they see it but who will do what you say because you have all of the tools to make your decision. Low-ball ten times in a row with no contract, and you may be finding a new agent, but it's your call.

I consider myself a consultant to my clients, not a salesman. I don't sell homes. I help buyers locate all the homes in their chosen area that seem to meet their needs and price range. Then we sit down and go through them with a CMA (comparative market analysis) weighing the pros and cons and comparing their value. We go back and look again at the short-list candidates, taking our examination to a higher level and being more critical. It's all about helping my buyers gather every bit of information out there about homes they're considering, then allowing them to make informed decisions.

$-$ 30 $-$
A buyer's agent should always give you a CMA

A CMA is a comparative or competitive market analysis, depending on whom you ask. It is always done for a seller, as it is an analysis of the market to see what homes recently sold for that are comparable to the home to be listed, and to see what is listed now as competition. This is how the listing broker and the seller decide on the listing price.

A CMA isn't done by some buyer agents, simply because the buyer doesn't know about it or request it. You now know about it, so ask for it. And you can ask about it before you select an agent. When you're working through those Web sites and getting to know agents, you'll begin to zero in on one or more of them. When you decide to make an offer, just ask if you're going to get a CMA. If you're told you don't need one, run, don't walk, to another agent.

To do a CMA, the agent takes a number of recently sold properties with very similar characteristics to the home you're considering, and adjusts their sold prices based on the differences in the properties. If the home you like has two bedrooms, and another very similar home sold recently but had three, there would be a dollar amount subtracted from that sold price to adjust for the extra bedroom. All features are compared and adjustments made. The comparable homes should be in the same neighborhood or as close as possible, and the sold dates should be as recent as possible.

Once this is done, a half dozen or more comparable reports can give you a really good idea of where the home you're considering sits in the group, and what a fair price might be to pay for it. But don't stop there. Also study the competing close-by listed comparable homes, and see where yours sits in the listing price pack. A lot of competition, meaning a large number of close-by comparable listings, could signal a lower offer because the seller has heavy competition.

Now you have the information you need to make a price-offer decision.

~ 31 ~
Buyer agency agreements: should you sign one?

A buyer agency agreement or buyer representation agreement is a commitment to work with an agent for a specific period of time in a certain area in your search for a home. It promises them a commission when you find one, no matter how you find it.

What they're promising to do

The agent is committing to locate and show you as many properties as possible that meet your needs and, within reason, fit into your affordable window. These could include FSBO (For Sale by Owner) homes.

What you're promising to do

You are promising that you'll only work with this agent and that he'll get paid. This agreement applies even if you find the home you buy on Craigslist before the agent found it on the MLS. There will be a protective time period clause covering the agent if you buy one of the homes you viewed together within a certain number of days or months after the agreement expires.

Example: You have signed one of these agreements with a buyer agent for three months, expiring on June 15. There is a protection period of three months, which would cover up until September 14. On August 20, you sign a deal to purchase one of the homes you looked at with the first agent. Even if you're working with another agent, this could result in a claim to the commission by the first agent, leaving your second agent with a headache and no money. Other clauses could change or do away with this situation, so you need to understand them if you sign a buyer brokerage agreement.

Whether you're urged to sign one of these agreements can be influenced by the market area, how much buying activity is going on, or in some cases, how good and how busy the agent is. If there are a lot of agents out there chasing very few buyers, you may be asked to sign one just to assure that the agent won't show you fifty homes only to have you jump ship. It's not an unreasonable request.

Some agents do have a good enough reputation and enough business that they can require this agreement. They then know they're getting paid and will work with you how you want for as long as you want. You can decide whether to lock yourself into an agent's services for the process if you're comfortable doing so. Remember that they're almost always being paid from the seller's commission.

There are pros and cons for both parties involved. The agent still isn't guaranteed a payday, as you might not buy. You may think you've found the right person only to be unhappy in a few weeks. Some really sharp agents will want the agreement but have a cancel clause if you're not happy for valid reasons.

The reality of this business is that probably less than one out of ten agents will even bring up a buyer

– 32 –

If you have a buyer agent, make sure to tell other agents

Especially if you've signed a buyer agency agreement, many agents are fine with you going out on your own to visit open houses. If you're into seeing everything on the market within ten square miles, they'll be happy if you don't make them haul you to all of those homes.

Whether you've signed a buyer agency agreement or not, *always* tell agents at open houses that you are working with an agent. Most agents only hold open houses to meet buyers as they're well aware that only a tiny percentage of homes are bought that were first seen at an open house. So they're sitting there waiting for you as a potential buyer they can work with.

If you're attending open houses and don't have a buyer agent, still indicate that you do. The best approach is to tell them that you're out looking at a number of homes, and that you're already working with someone. If you like them, and you haven't made a representation decision, you can take their card, do some research, and call them back. But don't get into a situation with an agent just because they're sitting there. You haven't had a chance to research this agent, check out their references, look at their Web site, or anything else. It's just a chance meeting because you walked into the home.

— 33 —

Sit on the furniture in staged homes

I don't want to dwell on this item, but it does happen. There are staging companies that actually advertise to their real estate agent clients that they can make rooms look larger with "creative" staging techniques. One of those just happens to be undersized furniture.

What this amounts to is a sofa that's several inches smaller than a normal sofa, and smaller front-to-back as well. When placed in the living room, it doesn't take up as much space, making the room look larger. It's not about "fake" furniture but more about "faking you out" about the size of the room. Once your full-size sofa, coffee table, and end tables are in the room, suddenly it's not nearly as spacious.

This staging can be set up in kitchens, bedrooms, and dining areas as well. In the grand scheme of things, it's not a huge and terrible thing, nor that common. But you're about to purchase the single biggest asset in your financial life at this point. Any manipulation of your perception of the structure or the size of rooms is important to know.

So sit on that sofa and see if it feels right.

– 34 –

When you're getting close, go see it again . . . and again

Moderation is good in all things, and you shouldn't abuse your helpful real estate professional by making her show you every home more than once. But once you're zeroing in on the short list, go back and see them again. The shorter the list, the easier to make a third or fourth visit.

Each time you enter the home, you are more likely to see something you missed on a prior visit. You've already been swept away by the modern kitchen, and now you can look at the bathrooms a little closer. Take notes, and make it a point to look at something different or in a different way than on the last visit.

I would much rather accompany a buyer three or more times to the home they decide to buy than to have them experience buyer remorse because they didn't carefully examine the home and consider their decision.

− 35 −
Is a bid war for you?

Although the mortgage and home-price problems beginning in 2007 ended a lot of "bid war" activity, it's far from dead. Whether the property's in the most desirable area of town, or few homes in an area are listed, there are plenty of reasons for multiple buyers to be interested in one property at the same time.

Though it's not a common practice, there are also listings that are purposely put on the market at lower prices than the owner will accept. The strategy is to stimulate interest and then pit the buyers against each other. It does work—this strategy frequently results in a purchase price at or higher than the realistic value, but sold a lot quicker due to the bidding factor.

It's a human character trait: we want what we can't have. So when we see what looks like a great bargain on a home in the best neighborhood in town, we want it. When other buyers try to take it from us, the tendency is to bid against them and get it at any reasonable cost. Their higher bid simply reinforces our belief that the property is worth more, so we raise our bid.

Sorry, but it's rarely true that you'll end up with an appreciating asset as the winner of a home bidding war. It's likely that you will have paid the very top price, or even more than the property is worth, in the excitement of the process. It could take years to get back to true value.

If you're interested in a home, and you find out that there's already an offer, it's not the best bet to submit a backup offer either. That's assuming that this isn't the *only* home in the area that meets your needs. Have your agent keep up with the progress of the deal and let you know if it falls through, but go ahead and keep looking for your home. If you do submit a backup offer, have it set up such that you can withdraw it at any time, leaving you in a position to look elsewhere. And don't forget that the offer's there—you don't want to suddenly find that you've made offers on two homes, and they've both been accepted.

36

The C.L.U.E. to a home's history

If it's not offered, and it probably won't be, you may want to ask for a C.L.U.E. report on an existing home, especially if it's older. C.L.U.E. stands for Comprehensive Loss Underwriting Exchange, which gives a history of any insurance losses paid on a home in the last five years.

With mold being a high-profile problem, it would be important to know whether there has been extensive water damage in a home that resulted in an insurance payment for correction. Something recent could also make it difficult or impossible for you to get insurance. It's just good sense to check on the insurance-claim history of an investment as large as this. The good news is that it's less than $20 for the report, so you're not asking the seller for a big concession. And they can use it again if you decide to move on to purchasing another home.

Once you're at the point of writing the contract, have a contingency put in for delivery of a C.L.U.E. report, with time for your review, and the deal will continue only if there's nothing scary in there. It can be ordered online (but only by the owner) for fast delivery at www.choicetrust.com.

37

What your agent *must* disclose to you

Depending on their laws, most states require an agent to disclose any "material facts" they know about the home or the sale. There are some gray areas in "material," but it generally means anything that would have caused you not to make an offer in the first place, or to make a lower offer had you known about it.

There are also fair housing laws that are federal, and some more restrictive state laws. So if your agent tells you that he can't talk about something, then he probably can't. An example would be a suicide in the home. It's required to be disclosed in some states, and could be against the law to disclose in others. But if the agent knows about a structural problem or something wrong with the property, or later sees a problem, he must make sure that you know about it.

For example, I showed a home with a huge crack in the living room slab, right through the tile. This was a really wide, deep crack. My clients didn't buy, and I ended up showing the same home again a few months later. At that point there was no tile but new wall-to-wall carpeting. I disclosed what I knew about the damage, even though the owners may have repaired the crack under all that carpet padding.

— 38 —
The property disclosure

Most states require house sellers to complete a property condition disclosure form. This form usually has a long list of questions or condition items which prompt the seller to fill in what they know about problems with the home, equipment, structures, or even ownership or title.

Of course, it is signed by the seller who is supposed to tell the truth, the whole truth, and nothing but the truth. Generally, you can assume mostly truthful statements. There's more of an issue, however, in items not answered at all. Even though I know agents tell sellers to answer all questions, with "I don't know" being an acceptable answer, there still end up being unanswered items.

Don't accept this. If you decide to make an offer on a home and you've already seen a disclosure with blanks in it, make a condition in the offer that you get answers to those items, if they apply. Obviously, basement questions for a home with no basement would not be something you should argue about. If you don't see the disclosure until after a deal, there are methods to object to items that your agent can help you with. It's then a matter of requiring that the seller fill in the blanks so you have the information to continue with the deal.

Never hesitate to ask for more information if it's about something important. And get it in writing. If there's a major problem later, telling the judge "they said" isn't going to hold the water that a signed document will. Now may be a good time to mention that it's almost never to your benefit to hear "verbal is okay" in a deal. Get it in writing!

Lead base paint in homes built before 1978

Lead base paint is present in a large percentage of unremodeled homes built prior to 1978, when it was made illegal due to health hazards. Tens of millions of homes have or did have lead base paint, many in every room. The health hazards were great enough, especially to children, that the EPA developed a special disclosure for homes built prior to 1978.

The owner of a home built before 1978 must provide this LBP (lead base paint) disclosure to the buyer *before* an offer is made on the property. If it's not dated and time verified as having been signed by the buyers prior to the offer to purchase, stiff fines are in place for the brokers and agents involved.

It's important for you as the buyer to get this LBP disclosure early and sign off before going forward with a purchase contract. Generally, that's the way it's handled. But if you're looking at a home that's obviously built pre-1978, or you think it was, and nobody has given you this disclosure, ask about it.

Some would say it's a lot of hoopla about nothing, simply because almost every one of the disclosures says that the owner is unaware of lead base paint in the home, nor do they have any reports or documents that would state that there is or has been. Hoopla or not, it's the law, and the EPA is serious about it. In fact, you're also supposed to sign on that disclosure that you've received an EPA pamphlet about the dangers of lead in the home. Both the disclosure and the pamphlet are required to be in your possession before an offer is made.

Once you have both, then you simply either waive the right to inspect for lead base paint or you indicate on the form that you want a period of time to do a risk assessment. It's your decision at this point, and you may not care, or you may care a lot if you have young children. If there have been multiple owners, there could be multiple layers of latex or other paint covering lead base paint.

In mid-2010, the EPA initiated new and stricter rules about lead base paint. Remodeling or other work that is done in a home built prior to 1978 now requires special work procedures and certification, thus a higher cost. Consider this if you're about to buy an older home and plan to remodel it.

– 40 –

Getting environmental information

W e're all concerned about our planet, the air quality, and the environment in which we live. If you're about to commit to residing in an area for years into the future, it's a good idea to know that you're not moving into a hazardous situation. The government at EPA.gov has a huge amount of information by zip code about:

- Radon gas, an odorless, invisible, cancer-causing gas emanating from the earth through foundations and into basements. Some areas have really high concentrations, and you should know if your new home is in one of them.
- Other air quality issues and pollutants.

- Water concerns, particularly well water from both private and community wells.
- Known sites that have been reported and are subject to environmental cleanup or special rules due to previous use.
- Even locations of previous underground tanks that could present a hazard in the future.

It's all there at EPA.gov, and it's free, so why not do a few quick searches to do what you can to be sure you're going to be breathing the best air and drinking the cleanest water possible?

− 41 −

Listen to your agent,
but the offer price is your decision

I've already stressed that you're the boss, and your agent is there to advise you. Listen to him, as he does this every day, and has likely bumped into most every situation that your deal can conjure up. But one of the questions even experienced buyers often ask is, "What should I make for a first offer?"

"Whatever you want to offer," is the simple answer. If you're willing to walk away and find another home, a low-ball offer may be the way to go. But get feedback from your agent. Who is the seller? People who are more likely to be offended by a low offer are owners of their first home, one they've lovingly maintained for a while, and they've never sold one before. Also, older owners who have lived in a home for many years may take offense to a low offer. If they refuse to counter your offer, it's unlikely you can come back later with a new one, unless you change your name.

If it's a foreclosure, or a builder holding a home that hasn't sold, or someone who has sold homes before, it's less likely that they'll give you your walking papers after a low offer. You may even get a counter offer $1 below asking . . . yes, I've seen it. They haven't slammed the door in your face, but they're telling you that it's only open a crack, and you need to get into their world with the price.

Try not to get emotional, and hope that their agent is telling them the same thing. It's a negotiation, and I've seen a dozen or more counter offers, with back-and-forth about not just price. One counter offer from a miffed seller stated that the low offer of the buyer would be acceptable, but only if the seller could take all of the light fixtures when they left.

– 42 –
Anything can be negotiated

Before you get to the point of making an offer on your first home, know that just about *anything* can be negotiated. It's "just about" because you can't negotiate illegal things. But almost everything else is fair game. If you want the hot tub that the listing says doesn't stay, put it in the offer as a condition, or "contingency" of sale. The worst that can happen is that the seller says no again in a counter offer.

Sometimes mentioning furniture and other personal property isn't allowed in a contract by a lender, as they don't want the value of the real estate muddied by extra items that can be carried off with ease. But if you want that storage building that the listing says goes with the seller, it's okay to ask for it.

Depending on lender restrictions, some closing costs, surveys, and other cost items in the closing can be negotiated. You can, if the lender will allow, ask that the seller pay some of your closing costs. If your agent says it's customary for you to pay for something, it may be true, but customary doesn't mean you can't be different.

You'll never know what you can get unless you ask. A couple of pages of contingencies in a first offer could just get you your walking papers. Negotiations require common sense and a balance of fairness and aggressiveness.

Negotiation with throw-away contingencies

A contingency is something that one side adds to the negotiation or contract that tells the other side that the deal will happen only if the contingency happens, or is met. The price is the most basic contingency, as you're telling the seller that you're not buying unless you can buy at a certain price. Of course, negotiations bring counter offers and changes. But just about anything can be a contingency.

One strategy that may be available to you is to put contingencies into the offer that aren't that important to you. Let's use for example an outdoor portable storage building and a free-standing hot tub, neither of which are included in the listing as coming with the home as part of the sale. You don't really care because the hot tub is old, and you want a bigger one anyway. And you want the space where the storage building is for a garage or a garden. Neither of these items is that important to you in the deal. Asking for them in the first offer could help you in future counter offers. You ask for them, not letting on that you don't really care whether you get them or not. The seller counters with a price, and they may either give them up or put them back on their side in the counter offer. At this point, you could come back with a little lower counter offer and give up the two items you didn't care about anyway.

It's all about getting the deal you want without creating a really adversarial situation. If the deal gets done and everyone feels like they're a winner, the rest of the process should be smoother. Don't forget that there could still be repair negotiations.

– 44 –

How much earnest money?

There are other names for it, but earnest money is the money that is included with a contract to show the good faith of the buyer, and the intent in going through the deal all the way to closing. The lower the earnest money that might be forfeited if the buyer backs out, the easier it would be to do so. Sellers generally want more, while buyers want to offer less. You'll get full credit for this earnest money at closing, so it's still yours.

Listen to your agent in this regard, simply because area practices develop, and market conditions influence the best earnest money offer. If it's common practice in an area to offer 2 percent of the purchase price as earnest money, then offering half that can get you a counter offer requiring you bring more, or an outright rejection if there's competition for the property.

Again, you're the boss, but staying inside reasonable and common practices in earnest money deposits will serve you well. Too little could kill the deal, and too much is risking your money unnecessarily. It's important, as you will want to get all or most of this money back if the deal evaporates on you. Of course, if you just walk away for no good reason, the seller may be awarded your earnest money as "liquidated damages" to cover their damages from you doing so. If there's good reason, like a survey or title problem, the contract generally specifies that the buyer gets their earnest money refunded.

Before you get obligated, get your agent to explain the earnest money process, particularly what happens if there is any dispute over earnest money when a deal goes south. No matter what the contract says, there could be a dispute that ties up your money, and thus your ability to offer on another home.

In my state of New Mexico, the contract is pretty clear about when a buyer should get his earnest money returned, especially in cases of title problems. But that same contract specifies that no earnest money will be refunded by the title company until both sides sign a document telling the company how to distribute it. So even if the contract allows you to get it back, if the seller will not sign for you to get it all back, it's sitting in the title company's bank account until they receive that agreement.

~ 45 ~

Counter offers: they aren't just about price

Okay, you've settled on the home, and you've made an offer. It wasn't obscenely low, and you are expecting a counter offer from the seller. Acceptance of a first offer isn't something that happens a lot, unless it is at full price or close to it.

Depending on other aspects of your offer, like the earnest money deposit, down payment amount, and inclusion of a preapproval letter, you may get a counter offer that not only counters the offered price, but also one or more of these other items. If you did ask for that hot tub they wanted to take, they may take it back out of the deal with their counter offer.

It is likely that their agent is keeping them in the game, and this is all just back-and-forth to get to a place where both sides can feel like they've won something in the negotiation. I've seen the same hot tub change hands over and over again in counter offers, while the price kept bouncing around. It's all a negotiation, and any of the contingencies in the contract can be negotiated, and re-negotiated, and so on.

– 46 –

If you're tough on price,
be prepared for trade-offs later

Let's say that you've taken the advice in this book to heart, really gotten tough, and negotiated a really low price on the home. It's lower than the seller would have wanted, but you had them over a motivation barrel. All is great, but be prepared to hit a brick wall later if there's more to talk about.

Inspections are done, and there are some torn window screens and a few other things you're asking the seller to repair or replace. Lo and behold, they say *no!* That barrel you had them over made them a little testy. And they really are just getting enough out of the deal to make a move to another home.

Just remember that negotiations aren't over with the first contract. Repairs and other items crop up on the way to closing. When there's an unexpected extra cost to the seller to be negotiated, you may have to eat it if you have them up against a price wall already.

– 47 –

Don't bring the moving van too early

When it comes to short sales or foreclosure homes, all bets are off on time to close. Banks are making the sale decisions in these cases, so time must be added for the bureaucracy. But in straight deals on completed homes, either new or occupied by the owner sellers, your agent will suggest a contract closing date that will likely come to pass.

Even so, there are a whole lot of people involved doing things such as inspections, repairs, appraisals, and mortgage tasks. Any one of these areas can result in a delay. Your agent may tell you that end-of-month closings can be a problem, as it's the busiest time for lenders trying to push through loans to meet quotas and get bonuses.

Any of these delays can get you into trouble if you've locked your loan interest rate only until the original closing date. If delayed, you could lose your rate lock and end up paying many more thousands in interest over the life of the loan, or higher cash up front to buy a lock extension.

Be very sure about closing, funding, and occupancy before you pull up with a moving van and have nowhere to go if things don't happen on time. Add the extra moving truck costs to a hotel room, and your closing costs can jump.

Dates and deadlines do matter

Once there's a basic contract agreement, all kinds of delivery dates and deadlines kick in. Of course there's a closing date, but there are also a bunch of other dates that detail when all types of disclosures, documents, inspections, and surveys are due. Dates matter, although agents sometimes let them pass, and as long as the other side does nothing to cause a problem about it, then it's not a problem.

But missing even one delivery or response date can give the other side an "out" if they've become disenchanted with the deal, or if there's a backup offer in the picture. Don't rely on your agent to remember all dates; ask for a calendar or printout of all due dates in the contract. Don't feel a bit concerned about calling or texting the agent as a reminder of a date that's about to pass.

If it is agreed to let a date slide, or there's an agreed postponement, it needs to be in writing as it's an amendment to the contract. As previously mentioned, verbal promises don't hold much water.

– 49 –
The interest rate lock

Once you've come to a deal on a home and have signed the purchase contract, you'll be getting busy on a number of tasks. One is completing the loan application process and getting final approval for the mortgage. A closing date has been set up, though it could change if there are delays, and you are now seriously getting into the mortgage process.

No matter how stable interest rates appear to be, there could be an interest rate increase before you close the purchase. If rates are bouncing around, it's even more important to discuss locking in an interest rate with your lender. Generally, a rate can be locked in without extra cost for thirty days or so, but longer than that could carry a fee.

The lender is promising you that she'll honor the rate for that number of days, even if rates go up. Therefore, your rate and payment will be what you expect without a nasty surprise before closing.

— 50 —

With all of these professionals involved, mistakes don't happen . . . right?

W rong! I've seen everything from major property legal description errors to survey errors and just plain typos that could create annoying problems down the road. You should not sign a document that you haven't read or don't understand. It's just too big of a purchase and too important.

If you don't understand why something is the way it's written, ask about it. You're the customer, and the most important one, by the way! If you don't buy, they don't sell, and nobody gets paid. Never hesitate to ask about anything that you don't fully understand.

I won't go into detail about the true story of a closing and sale of the wrong piece of land to a

buyer, who came out two years later to find someone's home on what they thought was their land. It
happens.

– 51 –
Choosing a home inspector

Here's another area where an agent or mortgage broker who gives you this book should be given preference. If they want to guide you in the direction of a specific inspector or recommend one outright, they don't want to give you this book. Why? Because right here you're learning not to let any real estate agent, lender, or other involved party push you in the direction of a certain inspector.

A list of inspectors (the longer the better) might be all right. The point is to not let anyone who has an agenda enter into this decision. Like in any profession, there are bad apples in the real estate–agent barrel. Stories are out there about agents sending the buyer to an inspector known to be "easy," letting important things slide so the deal will go through.

This unprofessional method of referring inspectors is not common, and the vast majority of agents wouldn't think of doing this, nor would lenders. But you're the boss, so choose your inspector from a number of them after speaking to them about their procedures. This needs to be done quickly, as it's probably the first deadline item on your to-do list as a buyer.

Use an inspector with E&O (errors and omissions) insurance if possible. Nobody's perfect, and inspectors miss things sometimes. E&O insurance is their coverage for errors that cause you damage, property or monetary. It's there to protect them by compensating you to avoid a costly lawsuit. In some states this insurance is required, but a careful inspector will want this coverage even if they're not required by law to have it.

The inspector's shadow—
that's you

Even if they're willing or allowed to stay with an inspector, many agents will decline to do so if you're able to be there. There is too much liability, and some inspectors have actually accused agents of intimidating them by hanging over their shoulders. So you're the shoulder-hanger. And you should be.

Home inspectors have a list, and they work the list. They then create a written report of the list and what they find. It's a script of sorts for the inspection. There's nothing wrong with this method because they need a routine, but you need to take them off-script if there's something you see and don't understand. Follow, watch, and even take photos if they are not doing so. Whenever you see anything you don't understand, ask a question, even if it's a note the inspector makes. Make your own notes as well.

Later, if there's an error or if something you discussed isn't in the report, you can bring it up and get it corrected. You are the customer here. Your questions will get you more information than what may be written up in the report.

~ 53 ~
There may be multiple inspectors

Everyone can't be an expert at everything. Home inspectors are no different. Depending on location, climate, and other variables, there could be a number of specialty inspections. If mold is an issue in the area, this one might need to be examined by an inspector specializing in mold issues. Radon is another factor in some areas of the country. Wells and septic systems could also be involved.

Yes, you're paying for the inspection. So if you speak to a general home inspector who is licensed and experienced in doing all or most of the different inspections, then great, you'll get several done with one fee! But if there's an important item in question and the general inspector doesn't usually do that specific type of inspection, get an expert.

Here's when you may choose to take a specific recommendation for an inspector: from the general inspector. They have no agenda here, and they may know the best inspectors for each item simply because they've worked with them on other deals.

54

Homeowner's insurance

Another item you'll want to jump on right away after the contract is signed is applying for homeowner's insurance. It has become more difficult to get a policy, especially with insurers checking credit. There may be deadlines in the contract by which you must tell the seller in writing you are unable to get insurance. If you can't, you should be able to get your earnest money back if you meet this deadline.

Insurance companies are becoming more difficult to deal with, and I can best illustrate this with a real experience of one of my buyers. She chose a national company and set up insurance with no approval problems. The deal closed, and her first year's premium was paid out of closing. While she was moving in, a photographer stopped by and said the insurer sent him to take photos of the home. She let him do that, and all seemed well.

A week or so later, a letter from the insurance company stated that the home was cluttered with boxes and debris. Well, she was moving in! There was also a statement that some tree limbs were touching the roof in the backyard and needed to be cut back. First, she went by the insurance agent's office and gave them a bit of a hard time about the "clutter" comment, inviting them to come out now that she had finished unpacking to see that the boxes weren't permanent fixtures.

Then the limb cutting was put on her to-do list. A couple of weeks later, she found her chain saw and cut the limbs. The very same day, the policy was canceled by the insurer because there had been no proof submitted about the limbs being cut. A letter in the mail concerning this didn't get opened until later that day because she had been cutting the limbs.

Whenever insurance is canceled like this, the first thing the lender does is take out a very expensive temporary policy. It was all resolved in her case, but with a big hassle and a couple of nervous moments. First-time home buyers need to learn from her example that the insurer's documents need to be carefully read, and any requirements should be taken care of as soon as possible.

55

Title insurance and the title binder or title commitment

O ne of the first things that should be delivered to you after closing is a title insurance binder or commitment. As the name implies, it's a commitment from a title insurance company that binds them to provide you with title insurance. This insurance protects you against unforeseen claims against your ownership later. These could be in the form of a claim from someone else saying they really own the entire property, or, as happened to my father, a later next-door survey that caused a claim to take twelve feet off the side of his lot.

Your title insurance company will go to court for you in cases like this if your coverage includes survey accuracy. You must ask about what the title insurance will cover and may need to pay an additional premium to get survey or other coverage not included in a normal policy.

You'll get this title binder once the title insurer has done a thorough title search and researched the chain of title or ownership all the way back in history. (Well, not to the dinosaurs, but they'll get back to things like land grants from kings.) Getting this document assures you that there's been a thorough check to make sure that nobody will pop up in the future with a lien or a claim to ownership from before your purchase of this great home. It doesn't mean it won't happen, but it does mean that the title insurer will go to court to protect your interests and possibly compensate you for loss.

There will be a list of requirements in the binder that must be satisfied to make it final, usually routine requirements such as the previous mortgage being paid off, having a satisfactory survey, a valid deed to transfer ownership, and sometimes a deed from a previous spouse of the seller giving up any claim to ownership because of divorce.

There will also be a list of exceptions, items being excepted from the policy that won't be covered. "Not covered" means that you will not be covered if you want to sue or assert a right to use your property in a certain way if it's prohibited in one of these recorded documents. In other words, you can't make a claim against your policy later because you can't put a garage within ten feet of your property line when the recorded subdivision covenants specifically said you couldn't. Or if there is an easement for the electric company to bury a line along your property edge, you cannot make a claim if they do so. Usually these are known items in the chain of title that can't be changed, such as previous deed restrictions, subdivision covenants, and instructions from the king in the land grant.

There can also be items added or changed later in a "revised" title binder. This happens a lot after the survey. Anything noted on the survey could result in an exception. An example from my area is a dirt road track that Jeeps have been using to cross the property. The surveyor noted it, so the title company will except it, meaning they won't insure you against someone trying to use it again. If an encroachment is noted, such as the neighbor putting up a storage building that's one foot over the property line, it will be an exception. You may then object and have the seller get the neighbor to move it, and the neighbor may or may not. The exception just covers the title insurer either way.

The most important thing to remember here is that somebody needs to read this document carefully, and it should be you. Note questions, and get them answered by the agent or preferably the title company. There is little or nothing you can do if you close on the property then later find a problem like an easement for a billion-volt power line to be constructed over the center of your new home.

There will be a contractual time period for you to review the title binder, get questions answered, and make objections if necessary. Just know that there aren't many objections to items in a title binder that a seller has the power to correct. Most of them will be things mentioned in deeds, access easements, and other documents that are legally binding and can't be erased just because you don't like them. So in the unlikely event you have a strong objection to something in the title binder, it's probably going to kill the deal.

– 56 –
Easements

Easements are established to pass certain rights to non-owners of property to use or cross the property. An example in my area is the common driveway serving several properties off the main road. The properties on the way to the last home grant the homeowner at the end easements to cross their property for access to the main road.

Another common form of easement is the utility easement. Natural gas, electric, and phone companies all need to serve their customers with wires or pipes that are frequently buried underground. Thus, there are narrow strips of land along the edges between properties that are easements for power lines, as well as phone and gas lines. For example, if the easement is ten feet, five feet would generally be used from each of the adjoining lots.

The property owners still own this piece of ground but can't use it for many purposes. Anything permanent built there could be damaged or destroyed by the utility companies in exercising their rights to dig up that area to add or modify services. You'll want to know about these easements because if you don't, it's a real letdown for that brand-new concrete deck or driveway to be jackhammered to make a gas-line repair.

Easements are a very normal part of real estate ownership but can sometimes take on abnormal forms. I once had a property in the mountains that had an easement for a lady to cross it to get to the "spring of life," a very old artesian well. The well had long since been capped, and the easement was recorded in a deed more than fifty years before the capping. This was one case in which the title company actually took it off the exceptions list because they were very certain that this old lady was no longer living. A factor in that decision was the lack of any mention of the same right for any heirs in her estate.

– 57 –

Restrictions, covenants, and zoning

Zoning is a municipality's way of controlling the use of property to maintain property values and keep similar property types in the area. In other words, "residential" zoning would limit structures in that zoning area to homes, not commercial business-es. There are usually allowances for home offices but with strict usage rules, such as for parking.

Zoning tends to keep commercial separate from residential, and industrial properties away from everything else. It's good for property values and quality of life in most cases. Applications for zon-ing changes are constantly in the works, as well as requests for "variances" to allow a structure not currently permitted, such as a coffee shop wanting a residential corner lot.

When it comes to zoning, you should be careful to know the requirements for the area of the home you're buying, whether the home is in violation of those, and whether there are any major changes being proposed or requested.

Deed restrictions are common in my area, which is rural with few formal subdivisions. Thus, owners put restrictions in the deed on the use of the property that will pass along with ownership forever. They must, of course, be legal, but I've seen some weird ones, including how many trees could be cut to build and how those cut trees were to be disposed of.

Subdivision covenants and restrictions are far more common than deed restrictions. When a landowner or builder applies to subdivide land for building, a plan is required to show the proposed survey and lots. A very large document also sets out the covenants and restrictions for the subdivision. It can, and usually does, set requirements for maximum and minimum home square footage, maximum heights of structures, limit of animals that can be kept, uses of the homes, and much more.

Your title binder should come with all of these documents, and you'll want to be sure that you're not buying a home where your prized boat will be parked in the backyard when there's a restriction against doing just that. Or more upsetting, your prized pet potbellied pig isn't allowed as it's considered a farm animal.

– 58 –
Special condominium considerations

Condominiums are different from single-family homes in a number of ways. Most important is that you own no land with a condo. You're buying the space within your walls, and a share in the use of common areas like the grounds, parking, swimming pools, fitness rooms, and meeting or party areas.

Condos come with more restrictive covenants and documents as well as rules about behavior to protect the interests and peace of other residents. You do normally get certain services as part of your condo or homeowner dues, like trash collection, landscape maintenance, exterior structure mainte-nance, water, and sewer. And usually the exterior walls outward are insured, while you need to insure only the interior walls inward.

When examining condo documents and covenants, pay attention to any restrictions on resale. One may be a "first right of refusal" clause. This gives the condo association the first right to buy your condo at a price equal to an offer you may get from a third party. It's not necessarily a bad thing, but it throws delay and buyer concerns into the picture. A buyer who wants your condo could be discouraged to make an offer if the condo association can take the unit away from them. The good news is that these "first right" clauses usually require decisions within a pretty narrow period of time, but it could still be long enough to keep a buyer from making an offer or cause them to walk away from one.

Another restriction that could become a problem is one prohibiting renting out the unit. It's not common, but look for this. If you need to move and can't sell, renting out the unit may be your only option until you can sell. If there are restrictions on how you can rent it out, such as the length of lease, you need to know about them.

With all of the foreclosures and other mortgage problems in recent years, extra hassles have been created in getting a condo mortgage. Although they change, there have been extra lending restrictions placed on condo projects. If too many are unoccupied, there may not be a loan. If too many are owned by the same individual or business entity, again, there may be no loan. If too many are rented rather than owner-occupied, there could be problems with mortgages. It's very important for you to check with the mortgage broker you select on the current rules, then make sure that you're not wasting your time and enthusiasm in looking at units in projects that are unlikely to be able to get a mortgage approved. And it's worth considering at purchase how tough it may be to sell later.

— 59 —

What's a survey and what's not

Other than condominiums and some other special properties that don't have land ownership, some type of survey or variation of a survey will probably be required upon purchase. Buyers can be confused by surveying terms like ILR (Improvement Location Report) or ILC (Improvement Location Certificate). There are other terms meaning the same thing, so let's define them here.

A survey is expensive because the surveyor does more in the process and guarantees their results to the property owner, allowing them to use the survey for any purpose in the future. Because they're expensive, in most cases the title company and the seller who usually pays for the survey don't want or need a full survey. If there's been a full survey within the last ten years or so, you're more likely to be provided with an ILR, ILC, or whatever else they call it.

ILRs look just like a survey, but they're a lot cheaper. They're cheaper because the surveyor doesn't do a full boundary survey and is working only for the title insurer, and you can't use it like a survey, holding the surveyor liable. This dramatically cuts the cost and shortens the time frame as well. If every closing required a survey, we'd all be waiting six months or so for a closing. So the surveyor does an ILR, drawing the location of any structures or other things on the land.

The title insurer takes this ILR, and if there's anything there they didn't know about in their title search, like the jeep track previously mentioned, they'll issue a revised title binder to except that item. This is also where that neighbor's storage building encroachment will show up.

Whether a survey or an ILR, your interest is to get that title insurance, which insures its accuracy. If another neighbor later proves this ILR and the survey wrong and wants to take five feet off the side of your lot, the title insurer should defend you or compensate you if you lose.

– 60 –

What if the home you're buying encroaches on another property?

Though not common at all, I have had a couple of situations in established subdivisions where the property to be purchased was found in the survey or ILR to be encroaching on the neighbor's property. In an easy case, it was a storage building on a portable foundation about a foot into the neighbor's land, so it was just moved prior to closing.

In the tougher situation, it was an older subdivision, and a fence had been built by the neighbor many years before, obviously on what they thought was their property line. The owner of the house my client was buying had done a room addition. The survey showed that six inches of the entire wall of the addition were actually on the neighbor's property, as they had the fence in the wrong place.

Though there could have been lawyers and fighting involved, the seller simply asked their neighbor how much it was going to cost to get that six inches, plus a foot-and-a-half for walking access deeded to them before closing. $7,500 later, it was done and the deal closed. So unless it's a huge encroachment or the neighbors are not reasonable, there is usually a solution. And it's not your problem to resolve the situation. You're sitting back with your loan and down payment waiting to get what you should in the deal.

Of course, if the encroachment changes the nature of the property enough that you no longer want it, then you should exercise your right to get out of the deal with your earnest money refunded.

– 61 –

Repair negotiations
after the inspection

Assuming you didn't take away every dollar the seller had to spare in the home price negotiations, here's an opportunity to get them to correct some or all of the problems that turned up in the inspection. This is one area in which contracts die, so you'll want to balance your desire for a perfect home with the fact that you could be out of a deal altogether if your demands aren't acceptable to the seller.

Each state has different forms, but there will be a document that is provided to the seller with a copy of the inspection. This is your "objections" document, or by any other name, the place where you tell them what you'd like them to fix in the way of inspection items. You don't have to ask for everything, or anything, but you may want some work done. Depending on the lender and whether the inspection is provided to them, there may be some items that the lender will want repaired.

There's one thing to remember here that's a human nature issue. If you require repairs, and the buyer agrees, their goal is a bit different from yours. You want a lasting and quality repair. They want to spend as little as possible. These are goals that rarely produce the same result. You should require your inspector to return after the repairs to make sure they are done properly, even if you have to pay the inspector for the trip.

As many deals do fall apart over repairs, have a clear idea of just how important it is for you to get this home, even if you have to make repairs yourself at your expense after closing. Sometimes you can have money placed in escrow or just paid to you at closing as a credit to make minor repairs. However, lenders sometimes kill this approach, not wanting to see any money passing from seller to buyer in the deal. One way around it, and a way to keep the deal on track, would be to escrow the money for contractors who have quoted the work and will do it just prior to closing, getting paid at closing.

Early questions to your lender can avoid problems in repairs and money for them. Find out from the lender what they will or will not allow before repair negotiations.

‒ 62 ‒
The appraisal

Especially after the mortgage crisis in recent years, there has been a great deal of government focus on the appraisal process. Many blame inflated appraisals for a lot of the problems because appraisers worked for the lenders and didn't want to kill deals. Lenders were also accused of pushing appraisers to find sold properties to validate the value necessary to get those loans done, whether accurate or not.

The much-criticized HVCC, Home Valuation Code of Conduct, may still be around when you read this, but it was also an attempt to bring more accuracy and ethical behavior to the appraisal process. Your concern should be the same as that of the people making these changes—an accurate appraisal that states the true value of the home. Even if your deal dies because the appraiser says the home isn't worth what you're going to pay, that's a good outcome for you because you don't want to pay more than it's worth.

A major change has been to stop lenders from choosing appraisers, requiring them to select from a wider pool, many times even working through third-party companies that gather bids from appraisers then assign them to the deals. This is supposed to keep lenders from using only appraisers who make loans work rather than accurately determining value. The problems many people are complaining about have to do with this new process, and also that appraisers from out of the area are being used and therefore do not know the local area well enough to do a precise valuation.

One excellent appraiser whom I know locally told me that you as a buyer should be there to meet the appraiser, see where they're from, and object to the lender if they are from far enough away that there is doubt as to their knowledge of your local market. I checked into this with a lender, and it was verified, at least to a degree: sometimes appraisers are scheduled and let into the property by the seller's broker, and you may not be informed of the appointment. So try to get with those involved and determine where the appraiser practices and whether it's not normally in the area where the home is located. It's anybody's guess whether your concerns will result in a different appraiser, but your objection could prompt the lender to check the comparable properties used, possibly resulting in a review appraisal to verify accuracy. In reality, you'll probably not be able to meet with the appraiser, or even be told when they'll be at the home. But you should be able to ask for and be given information about the areas where they do most of their work.

Many contracts give the seller the opportunity to keep the deal alive by reducing the price to the appraised value. If this is the case, you win by paying only what the home is worth. Be cautious and ask questions if appraisers change in the middle of the process. If a lender isn't happy with an appraisal, there could be an attempt to call in another more co-operative appraiser (though there are usually rules in place to avoid it). If you know an appraiser has been to the home then another is called in, ask what's going on.

There are cases when a second appraiser is legitimately called in. If a lender doesn't understand some portion of an appraisal or is concerned about the selection of the homes used as comparable sales, they may require a Review Appraisal. It can be just a review of the document and comparable properties selected, or it could be a field review requiring a trip to the property. This field review is especially important if there are plenty of comparable sold properties, and the lender is concerned that a different selection of comps would have produced a different result. Either way, it's in your best interests as well as those of the lender to be sure the appraisal is accurate.

Even if you did get a great deal, don't expect the appraisal to prove it

When the appraisal report is delivered, you'll want to check a couple of things. First, compare the square footage drawn by the appraiser to the footage you think you are buying. Second, check the appraised value to be sure that it's at least the selling price. Actually, the lender will be highly interested in this and will quickly inform you if the appraisal is low. But don't expect a much higher appraisal than the selling price.

Though there is a lot of documentation about the rules of appraisal, real-life experience yields one truth about value. In the vast majority of cases, the appraised value of the home will come out to exactly the agreed purchase price or maybe just a little bit more. That's of course assuming that it's not a low deal-killer.

No matter how many comparable sold properties you look at showing that you are buying the home at 20 percent below their values, don't expect the appraisal to show that. The reality of the appraisal business, and their customer lenders' motivations, is that there is little or no reason for an appraiser to value a property significantly over the selling price.

Look at it from their point of view. The lender wants the deal to work, and the appraiser wants more business from the lender. Nobody wants to do anything illegal or unethical, so if it's not worth the price, that's what the appraisal will usually say. But if it's worth 20 percent more, why would the appraiser want to say that? It isn't needed to get the deal done. They increase their risk because you may default at some point. If you do, when the lender forecloses and tries to get their money out of the deal, the more they lose, the harder they look at their appraiser on the purchase.

So while you and your realtor can rejoice and throw a party about your "instant equity" value over the purchase price, don't expect to see that in the appraisal. Should you wait six months and apply for refinancing, use the value you expected. In more cases than not, that's what the appraisal will show.

− 64 −

Changes usually require paperwork

A contract is a legal and binding agreement between the parties: you the buyer and the seller. If something changes about the basic contract, such as a deadline date or the closing date, it must be documented in writing, usually as an amendment to the contract.

Repair negotiations can cause a closing date to be too soon for work to be done. Moving the closing to accommodate repairs is fine, but it must be in writing somewhere, either in the repair negotiation documents or an amendment signed by both parties.

If the parties later agree that an item in the contract previously agreed to is now going to be different, then it should be documented with signatures somewhere. These changes happen all of the time, and it's no big deal. At least it isn't unless you end up in a dispute later and there's no written documentation of what happened.

– 65 –
Mediation before litigation

In many states, depending on the contracts they use, real estate agreements require mediation before litigation. This usually cuts costs, as the parties must mediate disputes before they can sue.

There are mediators who specialize in real estate disputes, and their fees are usually by the hour and high enough to spur the people involved to come to a resolution. A case when mediation, or just the threat of it, has been helpful is when buyers back out of deals for no good reason and demand all of their earnest money back. At the same time, the seller has costs and time involved with their home being off the market, so in many cases, they want all of the earnest money.

The money will not normally be released without a signed agreement as to how to do so, and who gets what. If there's a small amount of earnest money involved, like a couple thousand dollars, the money is often split to avoid the costs of mediation.

– 66 –
What if the seller balks for no good reason?

It's not as uncommon as you may think for a seller to suddenly decide that they don't want to sell you their home. They may try to come up with reasons that are valid, but if there aren't any, they could still just say no. You've met all of your responsibilities, paid for inspections and an appraisal, and suddenly you are told to get lost.

There is a legal concept called "specific performance" used in the real estate game to describe how a buyer or seller can sue the other to perform as they promised in the contract. In your case, this would be suing the seller to make them sell you the home like they promised. But that just isn't going to happen. Judges don't make people sell their homes.

What specific performance does do for you is to put you into a position to sue for damages. You've been damaged in that you have spent money and time in getting almost to the finish line, only to be denied your home without good reason. You have rights to try to get compensated for your trouble, mainly any and all expenses you have incurred in this deal.

We hope you never end up in this situation, but knowing your rights is important. Sometimes the threat of a suit is enough to convince the seller to go ahead and sell. If your contract requires mediation or arbitration, they may see a significant dollar outlay to make you whole, and decide that they can move after all.

The walk-through before closing

Don't minimize the importance of the walk-through just before the closing. Its purpose is to allow the buyer to make sure that they're getting the home they originally agreed to purchase, including all of the stuff they thought came with it, and in the condition it was in at the time of the contract.

Experiences I've had have shown me that people do all sorts of things we can't expect, and this inspection before closing is the last point at which you have the power to force changes to your benefit. Once you sign the papers, your power is mostly gone without a trip to the judge.

In one case, a seller took all of the doors out of the home; in another, it was built-in appliances. Never assume that you'll find what you bought. Do the walk-through. Take your original contract with you to refresh your memory about what you bought. And don't be afraid to stop the closing if things are not as expected.

– 68 –
Deed and legal description

A deed will be prepared, either by the title company or an attorney, that becomes your legally binding proof of ownership. This deed will be signed by the seller conveying the title to the property to you. It will be recorded in legal records at the county, and you'll receive a copy showing the county's stamp with the recording date.

This is a really important document, and you should review it prior to closing. But whether you do or not, I have seen errors in deeds more than once. It's not likely that you'll lose the property over it, but there will very likely be problems when you go to sell it. If there is a typo on the deed, it isn't legally describing your property. It can, and will, be corrected, but why let it happen in the first place?

Get a copy of the deed before or at closing. Compare the legal description of the property in the deed to the legal description in the survey and the title insurance policy binder. They should all be exactly the same. If not, a correction before closing is easier and less stressful.

Closing doesn't mean possession

Closing doesn't necessarily mean possession. Contracts in different states have various ways of handling this, but generally you'll get the keys when the seller gets the money. This is called "funding." Or you'll get the keys when the deed is recorded at the courthouse, called "recording." Since the title company will not record a deed until the seller has received their funding, recording requires funding. In other words, it must be a done deal before they let you take possession. It's not fair to try to talk your agent into getting the keys early, as it could jeopardize their license if they give them to you.

While most states are working their way to "table funding"—funding that's almost immediate following signing of the loan documents by the buyer—it may not be that quick. Usually though, my buyers get their keys the same day if we close before noon and the next morning if we don't. This gives the title company personnel the time to file the deed at the courthouse and verify that funds have been passed to the seller.

– 70 –
The closing

Though it's still done in some areas, usually the buyers and sellers never need to see each other in a transaction, including the closing. Each has their own paperwork to do and documents to sign, and one is getting money while you're paying it. So don't expect a sit-down with everyone at the table. It will probably just be the title company closing person, your agent, your mortgage broker, and you.

Bring whatever they tell you that you'll need, though it shouldn't be documents, as all of that will be there, including a large pile of loan docs. But you will need valid identification, as they need to make a copy of something like your driver's license to put in the file proving the real buyer actually signed everything. The title company person or another employee will be a notary, so everything will be completed on the spot and will be legal.

If you're bringing more money to go with your initial earnest money, you'll need a cashier's check or other guaranteed money instrument from the bank. You'll be given that amount, as well as seeing it on the HUD-1 Settlement Statement on the buyer side of the sheet. It will be explained to you, item by item, and you'll see where you're being given credit for your earnest money deposit, and the additions of all lender and other closing fees.

Your escrow amounts will be there as well. Technically, they're not closing costs but are really just prepaid taxes and insurance to fund your escrow account for payments made on your behalf.

Title personnel, real estate agents, and mortgage brokers do these closings all the time, but this is your first. Don't think twice about reading as much of that pile of documents as you need to in order to feel comfortable signing. Ask questions, and have them explain *every* line of the HUD-1 Settlement

Statement to you. If the closing takes longer than they anticipated, don't worry. Nobody in the room gets a paycheck until you sign on all of the dotted lines.

Conclusion

Buying your first home is an exciting and life-changing experience. It's best that the life-changing part be for the better. That's why knowledge of the process, and working with people who have no fear of educating you and letting you make informed decisions, is a must.

Everything you may bump into in your home search and transaction may not be in this book. Things may crop up in the negotiations or documents and title search that nobody could anticipate. But the real estate agents, mortgage brokers, title company personnel, and inspectors are all there to make this purchase work for you. Never hesitate to ask questions, and don't feel like you're imposing to ask them over again if you didn't understand the first answers.

I sincerely hope that this book helps you, if in no other way than giving you a greater comfort level from knowing that you have the information here to make informed decisions in your first-time home purchase.

Check out these other books in the
Good Things to Know series:

5 Things to Know for Successful and Lasting Weight Loss
(ISBN: 9781596525580, $9.99)
12 Things to Do to Quit Smoking
(ISBN: 9781596525849, $9.99)\
21 Things To Create a Better Life
(ISBN: 9781596525269, $9.99)
27 Things To Feng Shui Your Home
(ISBN: 9781596525672, $9.99)
27 Things To Know About Yoga
(ISBN: 9781596525900, $9.99)
29 Things To Know About Catholicism
(ISBN: 9781596525887, $9.99)
30 Things Future Dads Should Know About Pregnancy
(ISBN: 9781596525924, $9.99)
33 Things To Know About Raising Creative Kids
(ISBN: 9781596525627, $9.99)
34 Things To Know About Wine
(ISBN: 9781596525894, $9.99)

Printed in the USA
CPSIA information can be obtained
at www.ICGtesting.com
JSHW052016140824
68134JS00027B/2503